Rev. John's
Divine Love Plan

*For personal and world health, wealth,
happiness, peace and transformation.*

*The practical application of the
Law of Attraction at its highest frequency.*

John Wolcott Adams

Published by Golden Key Publications
P. O. Box 30989 – Phoenix, AZ 85046 USA

Books by John Wolcott Adams

Positively Alive!
How to Have 'Unexpected' Income
BE What You Are: LOVE
Thirty Days to a Better Life
Power Words for Prosperous Living
Prosper Now!
How I CAN Have Everything
Rev. John's Divine Love Plan
The Secret of Multiplied Money
Positive Prayer
NOW Power

Cover design by Patrice Agliata, cre8design@cox.net.

ISBN-978-0-9801676-2-7

PRINTED IN THE UNITED STATES OF AMERICA
10 9 8 7 6 5 4 3 2 1

Dedication . . .

This book is lovingly dedicated to Rev. Doina Marie Barkhaus, a beautiful expression of Divine Love. Thank you, Doina, for the love you are in this lifetime, and all the rest. You are special!

This book is also dedicated to the memory of Dr. Emma Smiley, who was a good friend and mentor. Emma inspired me to *Live Life Lovingly*, and was a wonderful, positive influence and supporter in my early years in the ministry. I shall always be grateful for her.

Acknowledgements . . .

My heartfelt thanks to *Marcie Scheffner* who so ably edited this book; to *Patrice Agliata*, graphic designer, (cre8design@cox.net) who graciously and expertly designed the cover, and to *Janice Winscot* who did so much to help make it come together. I am grateful for my prayer partners who faithfully keep with me in prayer for the many people who are inspired by my ministry.

Part One

Rev. John's
Divine Love Plan

John Wolcott Adams

Introduction . . .

I believe that we are meant to live together in peace and harmony on Mother Earth, and that Divine Love is the Golden Key to individual and world peace. The purpose of this book is to be a real source of inspiration for accomplishing this goal.

The *Divine Love Plan* was first offered as a year long series via e-mail. It consists of 52 Divine Love Lessons, which are in Part Two and presented here for your inspiration.

The best way to use this book is to read one Divine Love Lesson per week, preferably on Sunday or Monday. This will set a very positive tone for the whole week. Review each Lesson of The Plan during the week. Affirm and meditate on the Positive Prayer every day. Make a sincere effort to generate and radiate love by centering your thoughts on the presence of God within you.

Divine Love is the highest frequency of the Law of Attraction. The more love you generate and radiate, the happier, healthier, more peaceful and prosperous you are. When I speak of love, I mean Divine Love.

Love is of God and is God. It is imperative for your spiritual, physical, emotional and financial health to get intimately acquainted with God. This is more easily accomplished when you know that God as Love is always present, enfolding and permeating you.

You may have well-grounded faith in the universality of God's great presence and power; you may study to know Him as changeless good; you may have a keen realization of living, moving and having your being in God. And, you may seek to merge your life with God's ever-lasting life, and this is all good. However, it is when you know God as Love that you truly know Him. Then your life has the beautiful divine quality you are meant to experience. Your true quest is to consciously *BE* the Love that you are.

The intention of the *Divine Love Plan* is to empower you to be fully powered by Love so that you may more easily realize the fulfillment of your heart's desires and enjoy the wonderful life you are here to live. The Golden Key to the life you desire is in working *The Plan.*

John Wolcott Adams
Golden Key Ministry-Unity
P O Box 30989, Phoenix, AZ 85046 USA
RevJohn@GoldenKeyMinistry.com

1

LOVE:
The One Reality

The greatest need of the human self is for love. Whatever else you have – wealth, fame, education, all the material benefits, most of your desires fulfilled – without love you are empty. The need to express love is vital to your physical body to keep it running harmoniously. Love is like oil. Like a well-lubricated machine, a loved body is a happy body.

Have you ever gone into a home that was lacking in love? Who would want to stay in a consciousness of hate, criticism, fear, coldness, or negativity? When I have entered a home like that, if I could not immediately leave, I would bless the place with thoughts of love and affirm love, light and peace for that home and its occupants, and leave as soon as I could.

It is a good exercise when there is an appearance of illness or other in-harmony such as worry, depression or lack of money in a home, to

3

open the doors and windows and let fresh air blow through as you bless the place with copious amounts of love. Do it even if it's very cold. The whole place will liven up with new life. A definite change will come about in the home and in all who live there.

Love will change any negative condition into a positive one. If you have a relationship with another person whose behavior tends to be negative, such as temper tantrums, insisting on their own way, threats, criticism or abusive talk, very quietly love that person. By their behavior, they are asking for love.

The old teaching was that God is a kind of vengeful, record-keeping, often angry, human-like Being in the sky somewhere. This is unscientific, has no validity, and is simply not true. God is pure Love – Love Energy!

In the 1980s, physicist Carl Sagan, presented a series of programs on PBS TV called, "Cosmos." These were fascinating and enlightening shows. One profound thing Carl Sagan said was that after many years of research into the make-up of the earth and space including the farthest reaches of the universe it was concluded that, "We are made of the same 'star stuff' that all things are made of." He said that all is pure energy. There is really nothing else.

With this in mind, it is obvious, then, that since God is all there is and God is love, then this energy of which Carl Sagan spoke, is love. When you think about it, it feels good. It is wonderful to know that this great energy called love permeates you, me and everyone, the air we breathe, the ground we walk on, and the food we eat—everything!

How interesting it is to watch children respond to love. There was a time when I thought of myself as a good "disciplinarian" as far as my children were concerned. Love was inconsequential. Just set rules and try to make my children adhere to them. It took me a while to learn that there is a much easier way. Love is the way.

I learned that when there is enough real love expressed, discipline, as such, is rarely necessary. When one loves enough, an environment of trust, harmony and self-respect is created so that children respond naturally and positively. In other words, they have a positive environment in which they are free to grow and express their divine selves.

Rather than subjecting children to guilt or condemnation, by loving them they can more easily accept guidance in re-directing their thinking toward happier and more harmonious behavior.

Unfortunately, many parents lay guilt trips on their children. Some parents mistakenly believe they must watch them every minute and reprimand them for every little infraction of the rules set down for them. Some families are more like military establishments rather than loving homes where love, harmony, kindness, understanding and peace flourish. This is often an indication, not of misbehaving children, but misbehaving adults, who do not love themselves, have poor self-images, are insecure, and are not illumined to the reality of God (Love) indwelling themselves as well as their children.

In such a home, things can be turned around with just a little effort and a lot of love. Peace in the home, and in the world, springs from love-filled hearts. Fear cannot stay in a home that is filled with love.

Everything responds to love. A business responds to love. I once knew a businessman who had a failing business. When told to focus on love, he literally loved his business into a very prosperous condition.

Love is the highest form of "positive thinking." A "positive thinker" only fools himself if he believes he can have great faith but doesn't back it up with the great success energy of love.

Love is not permissiveness or weakness. Love is strong. There is strength in loving. Love enough and you will be strong – invincible. Nothing will be impossible to you. Love yourself and you will be divinely empowered. Love other people and you allow them to be what God wants them to be. Rather than trying to change others – especially your children – love them, but love yourself first. You will love the results!

≈ ≈ ≈

I Corinthians 13:1-13; 14:1

If I speak in the tongues of men and of angels, but have not love, I am a noisy gong or a clanging cymbal.

And if I have prophetic powers, and understand all mysteries and all knowledge, and if I have all faith, so as to remove mountains, but have not love, I am nothing.

If I give away all I have, and if I deliver my body to be burned, but have not love, I gain nothing.

Love is patient and kind; love is not jealous or boastful; it is not arrogant or rude.

Love does not insist on its own way; it is not irritable or resentful; it does not keep track of wrongs, but rejoices in the right.

Love bears all things, believes all things, hopes all things, endures all things.

Love never ends; as for prophecies, they will pass away; as for tongues, they will cease; as for knowledge, it will pass away.

For our knowledge is imperfect and our prophecy is imperfect; but when the perfect comes, the imperfect will pass away.

When I was a child, I spoke like a child, I thought like a child, I reasoned like a child; when I became a man, I gave up my childish ways.

For now we see in the mirror dimly, but then face to face. Now I know in part; then I shall understand fully, even as I have been fully understood.

So faith, hope, love abide, these three; but the greatest of these is love.

Make love your aim.

2

LOVE:
Your Golden Gate
of Paradise

Perfect love casts out fear.
The Golden Gate, Emmet Fox

LOVE is by far the most important thing of all. It is the Golden Gate of Paradise. Pray for an understanding of love, and meditate on it daily. It casts out fear. It is the fulfilling of the Law. It covers a multitude of sins. Love is absolutely invincible.

There is no difficulty that enough love will not conquer; no disease that enough love will not heal; no door that enough love will not open; no gulf that enough love will not bridge; no wall that enough love will not throw down; no sin that enough love will not redeem.

It makes no difference how deeply seated may be the trouble, how hopeless the outlook, how muddled the tangle, how great the mistake; a sufficient realization of love will dissolve it all. If only you could love enough, you would be the happiest and most powerful being in the world.

"God is love, and he who dwells in love dwells in God and God in him."

How love changed my life

There was a time, many years ago, when I was very unloving and unloved. I fought an inner battle with fear, anger and resentment. This had gone on for years. It was a very difficult time for me in that I couldn't get along with people, I didn't like myself, was unhappy, unhealthy, struggling financially, and thinking of just giving up.

The change really began when I was trying hard to establish the Unity In The Olympics Church in Port Angeles, Washington, shortly after being ordained as a Unity Minister. The "experts" had told me that I could not establish a Unity church there because it had never been done before in a city that small. But, it was something I *was guided* to do, and went ahead anyway. I had no idea how my faith would be tried – sometimes severally. Fortunately, I discovered the ultimate key to success, which I share with you here.

(The Church is still there and thriving, and many even smaller towns now have Unity churches.)

I was raised on fear. I was afraid of almost everything. Fear had created havoc in my thinking, my body, and life. Achievement seemed to be harder than it should have been.

I prayed often for a divine solution, and it finally came.

I found a big yellow card with *The Golden Gate* by Emmet Fox printed on it. I pinned it to a wall in the small office in my home where I could read it often. Sometimes, when I read *The Golden Gate*, I would cry because I didn't have a clue as to how it could really be true for me. Fear had blurred my vision and I could not see how love could possibly make things better, let alone do all that Emmet Fox said it did. When fear runs one's life, love is squeezed out.

Fortunately, I decided to put love to the test, to prove for myself what Emmet Fox wrote. I read *The Golden Gate* every day, often several times a day. I desperately wanted to have love change me, and my life. I ultimately learned that love is stronger than fear. Love *always* wins. There is no reality in fear. Only love is real.

11

I made a decision to really discover what love could do and invited love to have its way in my thinking, feelings, body and life. I gave it permission to do whatever it wanted to do in and through me. I often meditated on love using the statement: *"Divine love, manifest thyself in me."* (Charles Fillmore) (See page 47.)

Gradually, almost imperceptibly, love began to change me. It changed my consciousness. My attitude toward myself changed. Soon, I not only began to like myself, I started to love myself, which was a strange but very good feeling! Before, I was fearful of, and distant from, other people. Now I loved everybody – unconditionally! When I began Golden Key Ministry-Unity, in 1974, I made love the cornerstone and it is still the most important ingredient of this ministry.

Life is good! In fact, it is wonderful! After more than forty years, I still meditate regularly on Divine Love. You are invited to do the same. Love will change you; it will heal whatever needs healing in your mind, body, life and finances. Love really does open doors, bridge gaps, heal the "incurable", work miracles, and do the seemingly impossible. Love will heal your finances, your business. It will heal your personal relationships beginning with your relationship with yourself and with God. Actually, you and God are the same. God is love and you are all that God is. Therefore you are love!

Love is the answer to individual and world peace. It is miracle-creating power. It is the energy that pervades all that is, and God is all there is. Therefore love is all there is. Fear has no inherent value other than what you give it in your thinking. Of itself, fear is nothing. There is no value in entertaining nothing! Focus the great energy of your thinking on love and fear will dissolve and dissipate into the nothingness from whence it came.

Yes, love is your personal *Golden Gate of Paradise*, right here, now! From my own experience, I know that love will change your life in a most wonderful, even miraculous way, when you give it your full attention. (This was one of my main motivations in creating *The Divine Love Plan*.)

"The imperative thing for life, freedom and peace, is love. Love is life. Love is light. Love is all there is. When we love enough, we see correctly with an illumined consciousness and vision. Love is so good it is virtually incomprehensible, yet we can know, feel and *be* love. *The Golden Key is focusing our attention upon love. Love is the golden answer to everything. Love is life and what you are.*" (From the author's book, *BE What You Are: LOVE*)

Rev. John's Divine Love Plan

3

A Beautiful Story

A woman came out of her house and saw three old men with long white beards sitting in her front yard. She did not recognize them. She said, "I don't think I know you, but you must be hungry. Please come in and have something to eat."

"Is the man of the house at home?" they asked.

"No," she said. "He's out."

"Then we cannot come in," they replied.

In the evening when her husband came home, she told him what had happened. "Go tell them I am home and invite them in!"

The woman went out and invited the men in. "We do not go into a house together," they replied.

"Why is that?" She wanted to know.

One of the old men explained: "His name is Wealth," he said pointing to one of his friends, and pointing to the other one, he said, "His name is Success, and I am Love." Then he added, "Now go in and discuss with your husband which one of us you want in your home."

The woman went in and told her husband what they had said. Her husband was overjoyed. "How nice!", he said. Since that is the case, let us invite Wealth into our home. Let him come and fill our home with wealth!"

His wife disagreed. "My dear, why don't we invite Success?"

Their daughter-in-law was listening from a corner of the room. She jumped in with her own suggestion: "Wouldn't it not be better to invite Love? Our home would then be filled with love!"

"Let us heed our daughter-in-law's advice," said the husband to his wife. "Go and invite Love to be our guest."

The woman went out and asked the three old men, "Which one of you is Love? Please come in and be our guest."

Love got up and started walking toward the house. The other two men also got up and followed him. Surprised, the lady asked Wealth and Success: "I only invited Love. Why are you coming in?"

The old men replied together: "If you had invited Wealth or Success, the other two of us would've stayed out, but since you invited Love into your home, we go with him. Wherever there is Love, there is also Wealth and Success!"

LOVE Will Meet The Need
By Frank B. Whitney

When your heart is in despair,
Add more love unto your prayer;
   Love will meet the need.
When you find a rugged way,
When you have a long, hard day,
When for help you pray and pray,
   Love will meet the need.

When your heart is feeling fear,
When you wish that God were near,
   Love will meet the need.
Love will bring God close to you;
Love will help you in all you do;
Love will help you to be true;
   Love will meet the need.

God as Love will banish hate
If on Him you only wait;
   Love will meet the need.
All your needs will be supplied
If on Love you have relied;
Not a thing will be denied;
   Love will meet the need.

4

LOVE:
Your Greatest Power!

Charles Fillmore, co-founder of Unity School of Practical Christianity, wrote: "Love, in Divine Mind, is the idea of universal unity. In expression, love is the power that joins and binds in divine harmony, the universe and everything in it."

It is easy to see, then, that this is the key to humankind living peacefully on Mother Earth. It is natural for us to love and unnatural for us to not love. Love is the inclination of the Universe. When we make ourselves open and free channels for the expression of Divine Love, we become magnets for all of the goodness of God. We naturally attract to us all that is needed to make us happy and our lives complete.

If there is a need for healing, love heals. If there is a need for greater financial supply, love is the very substance of that desired increase. Love that is generated in consciousness will correct any

19

mistake and harmonize any troublesome relationship. In short, whatever you need or desire that is good, is supplied through the power of Divine Love moving in and through you. (To learn more about substance, refer to the author's book, *The Secret of Multiplied Money*.)

The intent of this book and *The Divine Love Plan*, as it has been through my ministry, is to help you understand and accept love as the greatest, most powerful force for good available to you. Love is the power – the only power – that will heal, bless, harmonize and prosper you. Love is your miracle-working power.

One time I received a letter from someone in California who beautifully demonstrated the power of love to heal and work miracles. She wrote that she and her daughter had visited an animal shelter although they had no plans for having another dog after their poodle died at 15 years. But, as she wrote: "I spotted this pitiful collie pup in a corner of a cell. It was filthy, with one ear drooping. She looked at me and I at her. My daughter said, 'Mother, don't get a dog like that, it will be too big.' But something seemed to 'click' with this pup and myself. I asked how much the cost would be. When I was told it was $32.50, I said I didn't have enough money and asked how long I had to get it. They told me the dog would be destroyed at 4:30 that afternoon.

"I drove all over, gathering money from my friends. At 3:30 p.m. I was back and got the dog! She smelled pretty bad, but she licked my neck and we became immediate friends! Taking her home, I bathed her three times and found a very pretty sable pup with beautiful brown eyes under all that grime. I named her Kellie.

"A week later, Kellie was ill so I took her to the vet who told me I had better not love the dog because it had distemper and would not live very long. I told the vet I would not accept that. Kellie was given shots and taken home. Six weeks later, with prayers for her, plus mega doses of Vitamin C, and MUCH LOVE, Kellie was well.

"The vet called the Director of Animals and told her about Kellie and me. We were asked to come and visit their department. This resulted in a free license, and the spaying charges were cancelled. They went crazy over Kellie, and me, too! She is the perfect dog – house broken and obedience trained. She stays in her pen during the day while I am away, quiet and happy. She is intelligent, too.

"I see this as a real demonstration of love and faith in God. I never once gave in to her (Kellie) not being perfect. I know God is in all and through all. Kellie and I are very happy with each other, and my daughter loves her, too. I am so grateful."

This surely does prove the great healing, miracle-working power of love. So many times this same kind of thing has been repeated over and over when it looked hopeless as though there was no use in even trying. But when you hold to the Truth that God is the only presence and power, do whatever is needed to help the healing process and let God (love) do the rest, this great Universal Power always makes things right.

5

Live Life Lovingly

There is a chapter of the same name in my *Positively Alive!* book. However, I thought it would be well to include a Live Life Lovingly chapter in this book because it is so important to me. The sooner humankind learns to live life lovingly the peace we pray for will be established.

I am absolutely convinced that our loving Father-God loves all of His children unconditionally and desires for us to live together in peace and harmony on Mother Earth. His intention for us is to get along with each other. In other words, Live Life Lovingly.

With this in mind, I asked some friends to tell me what *Live Life Lovingly* meant to them. Their perspective was important to me and I found their answers very interesting. The following are what some of them wrote.

"Each day, each experience in life is an opportunity to 'let only thoughts that bless dwell in my mind'. This love expands to every God-being, animal, bird, bug, flower, tree, raindrop, mountain, skyscraper, and our world." – Jana Ostrom, Montana

"Life is about relationships. To live life lovingly is simply to listen whole heartedly without feeling a need to respond except lovingly." – Rev. Cynthia Ragsdale, Minister, Inner Heart Center, Peoria, Arizona

"To live life lovingly means to live life from the divinity within you. Living life lovingly is to love all that is, unconditionally." – Carole Fogle, Arizona

"To me, to live life lovingly means to follow the advice found in I Cor. 16:14, 'Let all that you do be done in love.' Look beyond appearances and behold the Christ Presence, the Divinity in everyone." – Rev. Shirley Bowman, Unity Minister

"Live Life Lovingly means to embrace the entire spectrum of who we are – both gifts and challenges – in recognition that all aspects of our life's experience contributes to our uniqueness. To accept this and bring it into our daily life with gratitude and plenty of humor." – Diane Mandle – Excellent Tibetan Healing Bowls concert artist, California

"Live Life Lovingly is when Love is at the center of your universe and your life, so that everything revolves around Love. What you do for others and yourself comes from Love." – Barbara Moseley, Arizona

"To live life lovingly is to be loving any way that you can, be it a smile, a kind word, a helping hand, a prayer, or loving thoughts. It means not being hard on myself, or others. It means keeping my love-light shining." – Rev. Doina Marie Barkhaus, Arizona

"To live life lovingly is to recognize that each person is a light in the world. The next step is to encourage that light to shine forth in all its magnificent glory." – Janice Winscot, Arizona

"To demonstrate living life lovingly is to say 'I love you' out loud at least once each day to someone you do love. There is magic in these three words. Saying, 'I love you' is the most beautiful gift you can give to another. They are the most treasured words a person can hear." – Larry James, Relationship Coach and Author of *How to Really Love The One You're With*.

"Live Life Lovingly is an expression of my soul, my heart and mind that Life is Good. It is the way of satisfaction, peace and joy." – Sam Bowman, Missouri

"Live life lovingly is a very simple idea. Don't step on the ant when you're walking down the street, let the guy signaling to switch lanes get in ahead of you, smile and tell people 'good morning.'

And always hug the cat or dog before you leave for work." – Linda Shanstrom, Colorado

What does *Live Life Lovingly* mean to you? Write your answer in this space.

*   *   *

Dr. Emma Smiley, who was a Divine Science Minister in Victoria, British Columbia, is mentioned in some of my other books. Emma Smiley was a good friend and mentor, who taught me the value of living life lovingly. This coincided with my discovery of love being the answer to the many problems I faced and my salvation from the debilitating influence of fear, which had taken its toll on my body, my life and my relationships, as well as my finances.

Emma Smiley convinced me that treating myself and other people lovingly was of greatest importance. It took a while, but thankfully, I learned this to be true. Doing as Dr. Smiley taught proved to be of great value. She didn't just teach with words, but by her actions. Although that was many years ago, I do whatever I can to continue the legacy Emma Smiley left with me and so many other fortunate people on our planet.

*   *   *

The Divine Love Plan calls for action. As good as thinking on Love is, and generating it within, unless it is expressed, it does not live up to its potential. Like the constructing of a beautiful building, a Plan remains just a Plan until it is put to work. The Divine Love Plan is a blueprint for building a very happy and beautiful life. As you prayerfully follow The Plan, it comes to life through your loving actions. Then you naturally *Live Life Lovingly.*

Implementing The Plan is simple. You just work with it daily. But because it is simple, that doesn't mean it is not effective. The more you work with it, the greater value it is to you.

Action is the key. The following are practical ways to carry out The Plan. Allow the weekly lessons to support you.

Kindness – Perform gentle, considerate loving acts, often small in size, but big in love. Be kind to everything and everybody ... not just randomly, but often, every day. Be kind to you, first!

Appreciation – Express love in words of praise. Let others know you appreciate them, and you are truly grateful for them.

Encouragement – Lovingly assure others they have what it takes to succeed, that they *can* live their dreams and you lovingly support them in their quest.

Caring – Genuine thoughtfulness expressed in kind words, touch and service. Practice the Golden Rule. Treat others as you want others to treat you.

Harmony – Let Divine Love, the great harmonizer, flow through you into every life situation.

Friendliness – Lovingly accept others as they are; be helpful, listen, supportive and friendly.

Gratitude – Be genuinely thankful for everything. Let others know you are grateful for them and for what they do.

Joy – The surest sign of the Presence of God. Joy is having the delicious, uplifting feeling of God as Love. Smile a lot!

Helpfulness – Kindly do whatever you can to assist others in their quests. Lend a helpful hand. Speak kind, uplifting words.

Forgiveness – Give love to yourself and others. Forgiveness is freedom from hurts and resentments. Forgive and experience joy and peace.

Bless – Speak kind, positive words of truth; do kind, supportive things for others.

Patience – Lovingly wait, knowing that God is in charge, all is well and in Divine order.

Peacefulness – Practice the presence of God as peace; being inwardly calm. Be a peacemaker.

Beauty – Through the eyes of love see beauty everywhere ... in yourself and everyone. Enjoy creating beautiful surroundings. Revel in the magnificence of Mother Earth.

Generosity – Give without restriction. Let love flow with and as everything you give. Be generous in giving love, praise, appreciation and money.

Feeling – Feel the Love of God that you are, surrounding and enfolding you. The feeling of love can be described as delicious.

Value – Value yourself and everyone as wonderful creations of God. God is love.

Hugs – A warm exchange and sharing of love energy. It's delightful to be in each other's space. Hugs are healthy! Fun, too!

Fearlessness – Be the love that you are; confidently move forward in peace and faith. In love there is no fear. Confidently enjoy the life of freedom and peace you are here to live.

Grace – Graciously accept God's Love for you over and above what you may seem to merit.

Grace is God's gift of unconditional love for you. Gratefully accept and live free.

Love Unconditionally – Love without restrictions, accepting others as the divine creations they are, without judgment.

Dedication – Devote your time and energy to being God's special instrument of love, harmony, peace and goodwill. Follow through on your commitment to be and express the love that you are. Let your Love Light shine!

You may think of other ways to implement The Divine Love Plan. When love is truly alive in you, it will flow out in beautiful expression. Regardless of how many years you have been on Mother Earth, what you have done or not done, or your status in life, now is your time to *Live Life Lovingly!*

Let this book be your friendly companion for the next year. Let it reveal to you your own divine nature and accept that love is what you are. Someone once said, "Whatever the question, Love is the Answer." This is true. Prove it for yourself. Faithfully work The Plan and enjoy the exciting changes that are sure to come.

Part Two

The Plan

The Plan consists of 52 brief, but profound Divine Love Lessons.

Preceding each Lesson is a quotation, which is a vital part of The Plan and directly pertains to that Lesson. Following each Lesson is a Love Prosperity Prayer for you to declare daily, and to meditate upon.

You will find it very effective and more fun to invite one or more friends to meet with you each week to read and discuss the Lesson, and affirm the Love Positive Prayer for yourself and each other. By supporting each other in working The Plan, you will grow together in your understanding and practice of Divine Love.

With each affirmation you build a strong consciousness of love and create a growing awareness of the Presence of God as Love. Through this activity, your thinking and your life are changing in a very positive way.

Keeping faithful to The Plan for one year is sure to bring abundant blessings to you, your friends, and countless numbers of people around the world.

Now proceed with working The Plan and get ready for a wonderful year of growing and evolving in Divine Love. One day at a time, you are creating something beautiful – A New You!

Love is life. And if you miss love, you miss life. - Leo Buscaglia

Love and compassion are necessities, not luxuries. Without them humanity cannot survive. - Dalai Lama

When we come to the last moment of this lifetime, and we look back across it, the only thing that's going to matter is "What was the quality of our love?" - Richard Bach

There is only one path to Heaven. On Earth, we call it Love. - Karen Goldman

Divine Love,
the source of our love,
bestows itself like the sun.
Love is a sun!
Love is a glowing, radiant
cosmic force, a vital energy.

– Russell A. Kemp

Week #1

An Irresistible Magnet

The Truth is you are an irresistible magnet of Divine Love, mighty to attract the wealth of the Universe to you.

Like a magnet, you attract to you what you have the mental equivalent for. This is why it is essential to focus on Love. It is the highest frequency, radiates only the best and draws to you only the best. Therefore, you are wise to give a lot of attention to Love. In so doing, a wonderful change takes place within you and your life becomes brighter, healthier and happier.

This week's Love Positive Prayer: I am a magnet of Divine Love now irresistibly attracting to me the wealth of the Universe.

Speak (with feeling) this prayer several times in the morning and again at night.

*Love is
total commitment to life.
And why shouldn't it be?
Life is the activity that gives
love its expression.*

– J. Sig Paulson

Week #2

Be What You Are!

This week let's focus on the Truth that God is Love and you are made in the image and likeness of God. This means that you are a spiritual being composed of all that God is, primarily Love. You will find it highly beneficial to accept Love as your Real Self, and consciously BE what you are.

In Truth there is only one substance and that substance is Love. Accept that Love is the reality of your being. It's what makes you the magnificent child of God that you are!

This week's Love Positive Prayer: God is the reality of my being; therefore I am Love. I am now being the Love that I am!

Speak (with feeling) this prayer several times in the morning and again at night. Rejoice in this Truth every day!

*God is love
and the feeling of love
is unity with God.
Unity with God leads to unity
with all of his creatures.*

- J. Sig Paulson

Week #3

The Feeling of Love

The feeling of love links all of God's creation together in symphonic harmony – the symphony of Life. The feeling of love is light for your pathway. It brightens your interior and exterior and illumines your pathway making it easy to move through every day.

The feeling of love – Divine Love – mystically and magically draws to you the best people in the world. Then you make the delightful discovery that they are just like you! Love unites all of us together in harmony.

This week's Love Positive Prayer: My feeling of love unifies my mind with God attracting to me the best of people.

Speak (with feeling) this prayer several times in the morning and again at night. Rejoice in this Truth every day!

*When love is
your greatest weakness,
you will be the
strongest person
in the world.*

– Garman Wold

Week #4

Love Frees You From Fear!

This week's focus is on the reality of love and the nothingness of fear. Everything negative in your life such as illness, inharmony, lack or limitation, are the appearances of fear. If you fear you try to have something that is nothing. Fear is not of God. Love is. In Love there is no fear. To the degree that you fear you are not Love. In Truth, there is nothing to fear because Love is the one reality.

Love lets you be free from fear. Love enough and you will be happy and free!

This week's Love Positive Prayer: Giving my whole attention to being the Love that I am, I attract peace, happiness, harmony, and abundance.

Speak (with feeling) this prayer several times in the morning and again at night. Rejoice in this Truth every day!

*Universal Love
is not concerned
with "me and mine."
It is always longing
to give to us, to help us,
to protect us, heal us,
and prosperous us.*

— Russell A. Kemp

Week #5

Never Underestimate the Power of Love

LOVE is positively the very best and highest force for good in your life and in everyone's life. Love is your personal Golden Key to peace of mind, health, happiness, success and prosperity. Yes, love is your miracle-working power, too!

There is nothing in you or in the world, that enough love will not heal. Love makes everything right. Never underestimate the positive power of love. Prove this for yourself. Deliberately give all your attention to love and see what happens. Let love work its magic in your life!

This week's Love Positive Prayer: The miracle-power of Love is now working its magic in my life!

Speak this prayer several times in the morning, and again at night. Rejoice in this Truth every day.

God's love brings forth
the fulfillment
of all your needs.
There is nothing that
His love cannot fulfill!

– Rev. John – "Positively Alive!"

Week #6

Focus Completely on Love!

Wouldn't it be interesting to see what would happen if the Law of Love was fully and continually applied in the business world as well as in family and other human relationships?

Love never judges, never criticizes or condemns. Love is so slow to anger that it never gets around to it! Love understands, approves, harmonizes, perfects and prospers. Love heals everything and is the answer to every question.

This week let your focus be so much on Love there is no room for anything negative – only the positive, happy, lovely, and good. Remember: Love is the highest frequency of the Law of Attraction. Expect great things to happen. They are happening now!

This week's Love Positive Prayer: Focusing completely on Love, I am happy, healthy, prosperous, and free! Great things are happening to me!

Speak the above prayer several times in the morning and at night. Feel the love that you are and let it radiate to all people.

*There should be periods
of mental concentration
on love. Think about love,
and all the ideas that go
to make up love
will be set into motion.*

– Charles Fillmore

Week #7

Meditate on Divine Love

Charles Fillmore, co-founder of Unity, said to make it a daily practice to meditate on Divine Love with the statement: *"Divine Love, manifest thyself in me."* I have found this to be a powerful, life-changing practice. Try it for yourself.

Speak this week's Love Positive Prayer many times daily inviting Divine Love to manifest itself in your consciousness and whole being. If you will do this every day for one full week, I believe you will be delighted with the results.

This week's Love Positive Prayer: Divine Love, manifest thyself in me.

Speak (with feeling) this prayer several times in the morning and again at night. Speak these words into the silence and meditate on them, too.

*Remind yourself that
loving words and loving thoughts
are supercharged with
power to produce good.*

– Catherine Ponder

Week #8

Be Loving!

One of the essentials of Love – Divine Love – is lovingness. It is good to think about Love and very beneficial to meditate on it, but Love is too good to be kept within. When you are fully immersed in the Love that God is, it is virtually impossible to keep it to yourself.

Each day this week, give yourself permission to express more love and to be more loving. Let go and let Love be expressed through you in kind words and deeds, in genuine appreciation, compassion and gratitude. Direct this positive energy to those close to you, and to everyone on our planet.

This week's Love Positive Prayer: I am Divine Love in expression. I express what I am in loving kindness to everyone.

Speak the above prayer several times in the morning and at night.

*All people, circumstances,
events, and situations
are attracted to you
by the power of the thoughts
you are thinking.*

– Esther & Jerry Hicks

Week #9

Radiate Love!

Divine Love thoughts are the very highest, most healing and prospering you can entertain and vibrate with. The best part is that you can't keep them to yourself.

Whatever you vibrate with radiates from you to people around you and on to every person in the world, blessing everyone. You can see how this will help immensely to establish peace and harmony in the world, raise everyone's prosperity consciousness, and make for a world full of happier, healthier, more peaceful and prosperous people!

This week consciously and more profoundly think Divine Love Thoughts into your life and affairs and to everyone on Mother Earth.

This week's Love Positive Prayer: I radiate Divine Love into my life and affairs and to all people everywhere!

Speak (with feeling) this prayer several times in the morning and again at night.

*Everything is really
full of love for you.
The good that is for you
loves you as much
as you love it.*

– Emma Curtis Hopkins

Week #10

Send Out Love!

Whatever it is that you would like to see manifested in your life will respond more quickly to you when you give it all the love you can. When you do, you send out high love vibrations that latch on to, as-it-were, your desired good, and irresistibly draws it to you. Your desired good will love you in return.

This is the *Law of Attraction* at work. So if you would really have your heart's desire, love it with all your heart. Send strong love-signals to it. When you do, you will have your increased good, or something even better. It's a great system that works miracles. The Golden Key is in using it.

This week's Love Positive Prayer: I love my heart's desire with all my heart, and it is now flying to me on the wings of love.

Speak the above prayer several times in the morning and at night. All day, whenever you think of your heart's desire, radiate love to it.

*Only love can make you
happy and serene.
Only by understanding
what love is,
only by understanding
it is all there is,
only by learning to express
this allness can you find
what you seek.*

— LOVE by Mary

Week #11

Love is the Answer!

It is sometimes a mystery why so many people seek outside themselves for what they want when it is all within them. It is in all of us. The name of this allness is Love. That is because God is Love and in God there is everything. That is why Love is the ultimate answer to every question. It is the fulfillment of every good desire.

If you tend to fear or entertain a lack of faith, add more love to your faith. Accept that as a spiritual being, made in the likeness of God, you have all that God is – everything, which is all summed up in one grand word – Love! Understand this and you will know that only love can make you happy and give you real peace.

This week, remind yourself daily of the reality of the love that you are and deliberately give expression to your belief. I believe you will find the results delicious!

This week's Love Positive Prayer: Love is what I am. I am now being the Love that I am.

Speak the above prayer several times in the morning and at night. Give yourself permission to BE Love in expression.

*We must vibrate
with love
in thought, word, and act.*

– Charles Fillmore

Week #12

Let Your Love Light Shine!

Divine Love shines within you like the warm glow of a candle whose light can never be extinguished. In Truth, Love lights the very depths of your soul removing all shadows of doubt. As you let your love shine into the lives of other people, you help them to let their love light shine into the world.

Divine Love within you endures all things because it is the pure love that is God. Divine Love brings out the highest and best in you affecting all of your relationships in a very positive way. Love's intention for you is to be its golden light shining for all to see. Thus, you make your world and that of others brighter, healthier, happier and more peaceful.

This week's Love Positive Prayer: As the Love of God that I am, I let my light shine and brighten everyone's life.

Speak the above prayer several times in the morning and at night. Meditate on this Truth and BE the golden Light of Love that you are.

*Real love is selfless and
free from fear.
It pours itself out
upon the object of its affection,
without demanding any return.
Its joy is in the giving.*

– Florence Scovel Shinn

Week #13

Real Love

Pure, unselfish love attracts to itself its own. It does not make any demands. Real love never sets conditions. It never says, "If you will do this for me, I will love you." Neither does it withhold itself because someone doesn't measure up. There are no limitations to real love.

Real love sees the divine in everyone. In India, there was a brotherhood that never said "Good Morning" to each other. Rather, they greeted each other with, "I salute the Divinity in you." In other words, the love in each one saw only the perfection of another. Not only did they salute the divinity in every man, they did the same with wild animals in the jungle, and they were never harmed. They saw only God in every living thing.

Real love loves unconditionally. When you love as God loves, you are an irresistible magnet that attracts only the good; you are unlimited and free.

This week's Love Positive Prayer: I love all people, everything, and myself. I see only the divinity in everyone and me.

Speak the above prayer a few times in the morning and at night, and let the love freely flow

*For thousands of years
people have disbelieved
the promises of God
for the most extraordinary reason:
they were too good to be true.*

*So you have chosen
a lesser promise – a lesser love,
for the highest promise of God
proceeds from the highest love.*

– Neale Donald Walsh,
Conversations with God.

Week #14

Accept Love's Highest and Best!

If you would truly improve your life and make it like God intends for it to be, love is the way. Accept nothing less than love for when you do you accept only the best.

Could you be happier and healthier? Living and breathing love raises your body vibration to the highest level. No dis-ease can stay where there is enough love. To enjoy greater financial abundance, lift your consciousness as you invoke love in every aspect of your financial life.

Accept the promise of abundance that only love can fulfill. Again this week, vibrate with love and let it attract to you, the health, wealth and happiness that is rightfully yours.

This week's Love Positive Prayer: Every moment of every day, I vibrate with Love, and gratefully accept Love's highest and best.

Speak the above prayer several times in the morning and at night. Meditate on Divine Love.

*If you are not attracting
the good that you
desire in your life,
learn to express love;
become a radiating
center of love;
and you will find that
love, the divine magnet
within you,
will change your whole world.*

– Catherine Ponder

Week #15

Radiate Love!

You attract to you what you radiate. If you radiate criticism or you are irritable, you may expect to receive the same from others. The Golden Key is to fill your heart with love because then you cannot be critical or irritable.

Moreover, you will be divinely irresistible. You will attract to you loving, harmonious people and all kinds of happy experiences. Your prosperity level will rise, too.

If you want to make a positive change in your world, let love be the magnet that radiates and attracts only the loving best.

This week's Love Positive Prayer: I am a radiating center of Divine Love and I attract love's best to me.

Speak the above prayer a few times in the morning and at night, and let the love freely flow!

The feeling of love
is the spirit of truth
that ultimately leads us
into all the good
that has been prepared
for expression through us!

– J. Sig Paulson

Week #16

The Fulfilling Energy of Love!

All great religions unite in proclaiming that love is the energy that fulfills the law and expresses our own divine nature. Modern researchers who have studied the nature of man have come to the same conclusion. This is not surprising because there is nothing else that makes as much sense.

It is not enough to only educate your mind through revelations of truth; you must let your heart be educated by the feeling of love. It is the *feeling* of love that "casts out fear" and dissolves any feeling of separation from God. When you feel love, you feel God because God is love. Then unity is established between you, all people and all things. In this grand unity, you are fulfilled!

This week's Love Positive Prayer: My feeling of love unites me with God and all the great good God has for me!

Speak the above prayer several times in the morning and at night. Rejoice in the feeling of love all day, every day!

*Man is so created that
he cannot survive in health
and wellness without love.
We are created
in and of love.*

– Eric Butterworth

Week #17

Love - Divine Love!

Love – Divine Love – is the vital essence of all that is. Love is the life-force that makes you alive. It is the energy that permeates every cell of your body. In Truth, it is the only energy! You are wise to become intimately acquainted with the great energy of love to the extent that you know that love is truly what you are.

When you do this, you will realize the importance of accepting that your health and wellness are dependent upon your conscious unity with love. The greater your inner connection with love, the healthier and more vitally alive you are!

This week's Love Positive Prayer: Created in and of love, I am healthy and vitally alive!

Speak the above prayer several times in the morning and at night. Consciously BE the love that you are!

Love in Divine Mind
is the idea of universal unity.
In expression,
love is the power that
joins and binds
in divine harmony
the universe
and everything in it.

– Charles Fillmore

Week #18

Walk in Love!

Years ago there was a famous lion tamer named Clyde Beatty. He once made a provocative statement when he said, "You could walk through any jungle on earth and never be touched by any animal if you had love in your heart!"

Recently on television there were two men who lovingly raised a lion cub to maturity and then released it back to its natural jungle habitat. They went back two years later and the lion came out of the jungle to greet them with joy. The lion's mate was also at ease with them.

A consciousness of love is essential for peace amongst all humans and animals! Walk in Love!

This week's Love Positive Prayer: Loving myself and everything, I walk in love!

Speak the above prayer several times in the morning and at night. Consciously and deliberately walk in love!

Fear distorts our perception
and confuses us as to
what is going on.
Love is the total absence of fear.

– Gerald G. Jampolsky

Week #19

Love is Really Everything!

Many people are confused as to what is real. Although we sense there is more, we tend to settle for a reality that is based on feedback from our five senses, which is often faulty.

Our lives are more meaningful when we look to that which has no beginning and never ends. Only love fits this definition. Nothing else measures up.

Love never questions. Its natural state is not comparison and measurement, but extension and expansion. Love is really everything that is of value. Invite love to expand your consciousness and your life.

This week's Love Positive Prayer: Divine Love moving in and through me expands my consciousness and my life in wonderful ways!

Speak the above prayer several times in the morning and at night. Feel the reality of Love within you and in your world.

*You can love other people
only to the degree
that you love
and accept yourself.*

- Shakti Gawain

Week #20

Love and Accept Yourself!

We are all made of the same "stuff" which is nothing less than Love! The way to love yourself, and everyone else, is to know this Truth.

When you love and accept yourself, then it is easy to love and accept others in the same way. If you find it difficult to love other people, check up on your personal "love-esteem." Love and accept yourself as the wonderful child of God that you are. Then it will be easy to love and accept others.

This week's Love Positive Prayer: I love and accept myself and everyone as the wonderful children of God that we are!

Speak the above prayer several times in the morning and at night. Feel and accept yourself as the love that you are.

*If a man foolishly
does me wrong I will return
to him the protection
of my ungrudging love.
The more evil comes from him,
the more good shall go from me.*

– The Buddha

Week #21

Love Always Wins!

One time a man made a mistake publicly, for which a rather hypocritical woman colleague ridiculed him. In her "holier than thou" attitude, she voiced every fault she saw in him while completely ignoring his good qualities and loving nature.

Taking the lesson from that experience, the man maintained his peace and poise and refused to accept her condemnation. Instead he silently sent love to her and others who were involved. Before long the woman apologized to him and harmony was restored. Love always wins.

This week's Love Positive Prayer: Centered in Love, I always send the best to everyone.

Speak the above prayer several times in the morning and at night. Feel love and let it radiate it to everybody.

*God is love.
These are the greatest words
ever written or spoken.
To believe them;
to understand them;
to feel them as true
is one of the greatest things
that can ever happen
to anyone.*

– Adela Rogers St. Johns

Week #22

Love Never Condemns

A woman struggled for years under a load of guilt believing that because of things she had done she was unworthy of, and therefore, not entitled to prosperity.

Fortunately, she eventually learned that God is love and love never keeps track of wrongs and never condemns. Completely forgiving herself, she felt a new freedom and peace. She was soon guided to open a small shop, which was successful from day one because she filled it with love. It was the beginning of a very happy and prosperous life.

This week's Love Positive Prayer: God is Love. I know, understand, and feel this as true, and great things are happening to me now!

Speak the above prayer several times in the morning and at night. Feel the reality of love within you and give thanks for prosperity blessings coming to you now.

*Love is the way of releasing
from your thinking and your life,
fear and all of its nasty forms
of expression.
Love makes your life worthwhile,
buoyant and successful.*

– From: *BE What You Are: LOVE*
by John Wolcott Adams

Week #23

Consciously Live in Love!

When St. Paul said that love is the fulfilling of the law, he knew what he was talking about. He had learned through hard experience that trying to do things fearfully without love was not only fruitless, but very detrimental to his health.

When Jesus said that love is the greatest commandment, He knew this to be totally true. He had a deep inner connection with God, therefore, He was keenly aware of the power for happy, successful living especially in the area of living harmoniously with other members of our human family. He said to "go and do likewise."

This week's Love Positive Prayer: Consciously living in love, my life is buoyant, happy and successful!

Speak the above prayer several times in the morning and at night. Feel love and let it radiate into your surroundings.

*There is a power in you
that has never been fully released.
The power that moves the world
and governs the galaxies
is within you.*

- Dr. Joseph Murphy

Week #24

The Power Within You

The power that Joseph Murphy wrote about is Love. This all-conquering power is in everyone and is the only power out of which everything is made. It is simple. God is all there is, omnipotent and omniscient, and since God is love then love is the miracle-working power of God.

The possibilities of Love are limitless. Knowing this, never again say that you do not have what is needed for real happiness and a harmonious and successful life. It's all inside! It's inside you! Discover it now. Love, the power within you, wants to make your life glorious. Let it out into joyous expression.

This week's Love Positive Prayer: Love, the power within me, is now making my life happy, healthy, prosperous and free! Miracles are happening to me!

Speak the above prayer several times in the morning and at night. Let love sweep you on to a higher level of joyous, victorious living now.

*The man who has learned
to love all people
will find plenty of people
who will return that love.*

– Dr. Ernest Holmes

Week #25

Are You a Love Magnet?

L. Frank Baum wrote 14 books about Oz. In one of them Dorothy meets a remarkable character known as "The Shaggy Man," so called because of his shaggy appearance. Yet everyone loved him because he had a magical love magnet, and as long as he carried it, every living thing he met would love him.

You don't need a physical object to make you a magnet. All you need is a heart full of the love that you are and to let love radiate from you to every living thing. It makes no difference your outer appearance as long as unconditional love radiates from you. You will be a magical love magnet divinely irresistible to people who love you. You will attract great good to you, too.

This week's Love Positive Prayer: I am a magical love magnet now attracting loving people and every good thing to me.

Speak the above prayer several times in the morning and at night. Feel the love that you are and let it radiate to all people.

*Infinite love is a resource in us
that is natural to us,
as surely as life is natural
to the physical body.*

– Eric Butterworth

Week #26

Love is the Equalizer!

When your body is taxed by exertion, the heart pumps adrenalin into the system, and new energy is released. When you meet conflict or inharmony, you have a built-in love equalizer that surges in and through you, and a harmonizing solution comes forth.

Unfortunately, not everyone is able to let the creative force of love do the work it is designed for. Too often, when there is a need for love, the love-energy is turned down, or off. To withhold love in any challenging situation is impractical and self-destructive. But when you allow the equalizing energy of love to freely express, your life is happy and harmonious.

This week's Love Positive Prayer: Divine Love expressing in and through me makes my life happy and harmonious in every wonderful way.

Speak the above prayer several times in the morning and at night each day this week. Deliberately radiate love to everyone you meet.

*Unconditional love corresponds
to one of the deepest longings,
not only of the child,
but of every human being.*

– Erich Fromm

Week #27

Unconditional Love

The essential message of unconditional love is one of liberation: You can be whoever you are, express all your thoughts and feelings with total confidence. In other words, you are free to be yourself, and others are free to be who they are.

There is no judgment in unconditional love. Neither is their criticism or condemnation. In unconditional love there is patience and kindness. This is the love that God is and since you are made of what God is, you are love—unconditional love. Relax and let go and be free.

This week's Love Positive Prayer: I am the unconditional love God is, and I am happy and free!

Speak the above prayer several times in the morning and at night. Each day this week, feel unconditionally loved and love everyone the same.

*Love is knowing
that God is moving
in all humanity.*

– Sue Sikking

Week #28

Love Empowers You to Do Great Things!

Jesus knew that love empowers and allows you to do great things. He was not limited by customs, class differences, morals, and so-called evils. Jesus was bold because He knew that He and His Father were one. It was love that allowed Him to do the amazing things He did.

Jesus revealed that love is the fullness of life and He demonstrated this on many occasions. He said that we were to do likewise which means that we are to love as God loves – unconditionally. We are to be not only aware of the same power that Jesus demonstrated, but that we *are* that power: the Love that God is.

This week's Love Positive Prayer: I give thanks that Love is now moving through me, doing great things!

Speak the above prayer several times in the morning and at night. Feel the love that you are!

*Love is the greatest healing
and drawing power on earth.
It is the very reason for being.
Love is the sole impulse
for creation.
The whole Universe
is based upon it.*

– Ernest Holmes

Week #29

Love is Your Great Prospering Power!

If there is anything that will cause your prosperity to take a Quantum leap, it is love. Love is, far and away, the most powerful energy you can invoke or express for living prosperously. In fact it is the only thing that can make your prosperity worthwhile.

People who desire greater prosperity will use affirmations, focus on the laws and principles governing prosperity, and on money. They will display great faith and confidence, too. All of these are good, however, love should be the main focus. (From the author's book, *The Secret of Multiplied Money*)

This week's Love Prosperity Prayer: Letting Love be my main focus, I am beautifully prospered in every wonderful way.

Speak the above prayer several times, from your heart, in the morning and at night.

When we have divine love
for all humanity
our love calls forth
love from others.

– Evelyn Whitell

Week #30

Love Sees Only Perfection

"Take not account of evil." Many of us are glad that we do not talk evil; glad that we are too mannerly to join in neighbor's gossip. But how many of us think evil without speaking it?

True love thinks no evil, rejoices not in iniquity but rejoices in Truth. The truth is: Every man is God's perfect child, and if we can see through the mask we shall see the Christ in others, instead of the outward appearance of imperfection.

This week's Love Positive Prayer: Through Divine Love in me, I see only the perfection in others.

Speak the above prayer several times in the morning and at night. Feel love and let it radiate into your surroundings.

*Love is that mighty power,
that divine quality of God
that is expressing
through all mankind,
and cannot be suppressed
by any outside force.*

– Charles Fillmore

Week #31

Accept that Love is Expressing Through You!

It is one thing to think about love and another to accept that it is constantly flowing through you. But it is important for you to realize this. The Truth is, no external condition can hinder the expression of love through you. Rather, it is an incentive.

Do not be fearful of pouring out love on all the so-called evil of the world. It is calling for you to do just that. Use your great spiritual power to deny the appearance of evil, and to affirm the omnipotence of love and goodness. As you do, your personal world changes and you establish love as the reality on Mother Earth.

This week's Love Positive Prayer: Gratefully I accept love as my reality and freely I let it express through me.

Speak the above prayer several times in the morning and at night. Feel the love that you are and let it radiate to everyone.

*Hidden deep in
every human heart
is a spirit of Divine Love,
whose holy and
spotless essence
is undying and eternal.*

– James Allen

Week #32

Love is Eternal

Love is the Truth of man; it is that which belongs to God; that which is real and immortal. While everything else changes, love never does. Love is always the same; otherwise it could not be love. That is why it is so dependable to solve any and all problems.

To fully realize and live in this Love requires ceaseless diligence in the practice of right living. This means to always be kind, caring and compassionate; to be thoughtful, peaceful and for-giving. It also means to be gentle, patient, gracious and grateful. This not just some of the time, but *all* of the time!

This week's Love Positive Prayer: As Love, I am always kind, patient, peaceful and gracious.

Speak the above prayer several times in the morning and at night. Feel the love that you are and let it radiate into your surroundings.

Love has many faces.
Love is the cement
that binds us all together.

– Delia Sellers

Week #33

What is Love?

Love is like a soft, warm light, glowing in every atom of your being. It radiates into the farthest corners of your life experience. Love is God's gift to you. It is always within you as the very essence of your being. Love is your never-ending resource.

When you call love forth into expression, God lives more fully in you, through you, and as you. Perfect love is the love that God is. It is not human love, but the love of God expressing through you. When you consciously unite with the love that God is, it is inevitable that you *Live Life Lovingly*. (Adapted from: *Getting It Right This Time* by Delia Sellers)

This week's Love Positive Prayer: Love is my never-ending resource. Thankfully, I let it fully express through me.

Speak the above prayer several times in the morning and at night. Feel the love that you are and let it freely express through you.

*You know your life
is transformed when
you are able to maintain
a feeling of love.*

— White Eagle

Week #34

The Feeling of Love

While it is important to think about love and to think loving thoughts, it is the feeling of love that transforms. The feeling of love lifts you above whatever may be challenging you and gives you overcoming faith.

The feeling of love colors your world with beauty and awakens your finest qualities. It expresses the beauty of love to everyone lifting their spirits and sprinkling their lives with joy. Allow yourself to feel love and to consciously be the love that you are.

This week's Love Positive Prayer: The feeling of love lifts me on high and makes my life beautiful, happy and delightful!

Speak the above prayer several times in the morning and at night. Feel love and let love color your life with beauty.

Love is the central flame
of the universe,
no, the very fire itself.

– Ernest Holmes

Week #35

Love, the Essence of All That Is!

God's love fills the universe and all that is in it. Therefore, it is wise to love Mother Earth, the Sun, the Moon, the Sky, and the Stars, because they are all evidence of God's amazing creation. The love that God is flows in, around and through you and everything. It is the real essence of life.

This love restores, renews, and heals you now. It brings joy, happiness and harmony to every situation in your life. It gives you peace of mind and guides you to discover new ways of expressing this love in your life today. You love yourself, everybody and everything. Your heart sings with gratitude because you know that everything is the essence of love.

This week's Love Positive Prayer: I know that God's love is the essence of my life and all that is, and all is well.

Speak the above prayer several times in the morning and at night. Feel the love that you are and live like you believe it.

*Where there is fear
there cannot be love.
The best way to be free of fear
is to realize Divine Love.*

– Emmet Fox

Week #36

Divine Love

If you love God more than you love your sickness, grievance or lack, you will cause healing to take place more quickly. Divine Love never fails, however it is essential for you to realize that divine love must be in your own heart. It does not operate from outside.

If your prayers are not being fulfilled, it is probably because you are lacking a sense of love for self and everything. Practice love every day and listen to your thoughts and words, and pay attention to what you are doing so that nothing contrary to Divine Love is expressed in and through you.

This week's Love Positive Prayer: Divine Love, expressing in and through me, makes me happy and my life complete.

Speak the above prayer several times in the morning and at night. Feel love and consciously radiate it to everybody and everything.

Forgiveness is choosing to love.
It is the first skill
of self-giving love.
The weak can never forgive.
Forgiveness is the attribute
of the strong.

- Mohandas Gandhi

Week #37

How Strong Are You?

Usually, strength is measured in bodily terms. When we see someone do something that requires a lot of strength, we may say, "He is strong." However, strength measured in terms of forgiveness is the true test of strength because it is an indication of your skill at giving love.

Mohandas Gandhi said it is a sign of weakness to not forgive. The law of love requires that you forgive quickly and completely. In some cases, it may seem to require a lot of you, but when you let love flow as forgiveness, it is often amazing how easy it is and the rush of love-energy through you is delightful. Practice being strong by forgiving everything and everybody who needs to be forgiven by you, including you!

This week's Love Positive Prayer: Loving myself and all people, I quickly and fully forgive myself and everyone.

Speak the above prayer several times in the morning and at night. Feel love and let it freely express.

*Only love can make us happy,
and only we ourselves
can determine its presence
or absence in our hearts.*

– Marianne Williamson

Week #38

Happiness is an Inside Job!

It is interesting to note that many people seek outside themselves for things to make them happy. However, having found those things, their happiness, if it comes at all, doesn't fulfill their expectations. This is because happiness does not depend upon outer things. It always comes from the fountain of Love within.

Someone once said that a person can be as happy as he makes up his mind to be. This is true. Decide to continually drink from the fountain of Love within. This is your Golden Key to real happiness. Love fulfills every desire of your heart.

This week's Love Positive Prayer: Centered in Love, my happiness overflows!

Declare the above prayer several times in the morning and at night. Centered in love, feel its joy and let it have free expression.

*Everything is really
full of love for you.
The good that is for you
loves you as much
as you love it.*

– Emma Curtis Hopkins

Week #39

Love Puts Wings on Your Desires!

The good you desire will come flying to you when you love it with all your heart. Give the good you desire the love it deserves. You cannot afford to be indifferent. Not only will the desires of your heart be fulfilled when you passionately love them, people will be irresistibly attracted to you.

The greater good you seek is seeking you. Love it into your life by loving it before it arrives. Love opens all the doors and windows of rich supply. Love knows no limitations. Fill your heart with love and let it flow freely out into the universe and your life will be filled with abundant good.

This week's Love Positive Prayer: I love the good I seek. My greater good now comes flying to me on the wings of love.

Speak the above prayer several times in the morning and at night. Feel love and let it radiate out to everyone and everything.

*Love can win more battles
than fists or instruments
of destruction.
Love is your "secret weapon"
for successful results.*

– Catherine Ponder

Week #40

Divine Love
Heals, Harmonizes and Prospers!

There is nothing weak about Divine Love. Divine Love is the strongest, most powerful force in the universe. Divine Love is so strong, when invoked, it will heal and harmonize any inharmonious situation. Divine Love always brings forth perfect results.

In any undesirable situation, invoke the power of Divine Love. You may do this with other people. Declare that Divine Love is mightily at work. If you are experiencing a financial "lack attack," affirm that Divine Love is prospering you now. Enjoy the prosperous results!

This week's Love Positive Prayer: Divine Love is now healing, harmonizing and prospering every area of my life!

Declare the above prayer several times in the morning and at night. Centered in Divine Love, feel its healing, harmonizing and prospering power.

*Love, in Divine Mind,
is the idea
of universal unity.*

– Charles Fillmore

Week #41

Love is Your Mighty Power!

In expression, love is the power that joins everything together. Love is your harmonizing, constructive power. Its nature is to heal and build up. When love is active in your consciousness, it conserves substance, rebuilds and restores you and your world.

Love is the mighty power, the divine quality of God that continually expresses through all humankind. Declare that love is expressing through you and your environment now. As you do, you are free of fear, and given the strength and power to accomplish whatever you desire. Invite love to do its mighty work in you and your life now.

This week's Love Positive Prayer: God as love, fills me with new life. I am strengthened, healed and fully alive now!

Declare the above prayer several times in the morning and at night. Centered in love, feel its joy and let it have free expression.

*Some day, after we have
mastered the winds, the waves,
the tides, and gravity,
we will harness for God
the energies of Love,
and for the second time
in the history of the world
man will have discovered fire!*

– Teilhard De Chardin

Week #42

The Way of Unconditional Love

Love is our great equalizing, harmonizing power. Love in itself is blind, so-to-speak, in that it does not see faults and shortcomings.

When we love unconditionally, we do not think of ourselves as inferior or superior, but divinely equal, sharing the same Life and Universe. We are not concerned with being something we are not, something that has no lasting value. Love makes us real.

Unconditional love is the way of true peace, health, happiness and prosperity.

This week's Love Positive Prayer: Today I love as God loves, unconditionally.

Speak the above prayer several times in the morning and at night. Feel love and let it radiate out to everyone and everything.

*Love never leaves you
where it finds you . . . even as
it approves of you,
it improves you.*

– Rev. J. Sig Paulson

Week #43

The Activity of Love

When you freely allow love to have its way in your mind, body and affairs, everything is enhanced and made so much better. Love does not – cannot – condemn you. It loves you just for the sake of doing and being what it is.

The activity of love works mightily in your consciousness when invited to do so. First it improves your thinking and your sense of self-worth. Then it moves through you out into your world drawing to you all that is needed to make you happy and your life complete.

Love makes you a mighty magnet for true happiness, peace, and prosperity. Rejoice in this realization now.

This week's Love Positive Prayer: I now freely allow love to work its magic in my mind, body, life and affairs. And, it is doing so now.

Declare the above prayer several times in the morning and at night.

*Love is
what created the universe,
and
Love is what the universe
is created out of.*

— John Randolph Price

Week #44

The Pure Essence of Love!

Love is the thrust of all creation. It is Mind, and also the thoughts of Mind. The Infinite All is the pure essence of Love. Therefore, Love is all there is and out of this you and everything are created.

Accept this as Truth and live accordingly. Let this Truth be the prime motivator of your thoughts and actions. As you do, you experience the grand life God intended for you when He put you on Mother Earth. Joyfully and gratefully accept yourself as the divine being that you truly are.

This week's Love Positive Prayer: Love is what I am. Guided by Love, I am living life grandly and lovingly now!

Declare the above prayer several times in the morning and at night. Centered in love, feel its joy and let it have free expression.

*Where there is a
strong emotional link of
either love or hatred
there is likely to be a meeting.
Where there is a
strong link of genuine love
there is sure to be
a meeting.*

– Emmet Fox

Week #45

Will You Meet Your Friends or Relatives on the Other Side?

The so-called dead are very sensitive to your thoughts, so it is not beneficial for you to engage in excessive grieving. When you grieve, it is usually through a sense of loss, therefore, it is more for you than for the one who has passed on.

To assure meeting up with only those you want to meet again, destroy every hateful emotion toward anyone. Freely love your loved ones while they are here, and when they pass on, continue loving them, but without attachment. When it is your turn, you will surely meet up with them again.

This week's Love Positive Prayer: I freely love everyone without attachment.

Declare the above prayer several times in the morning and at night. Centered in love, feel the joy of it and freely express love.

*Hidden deep
in every human heart,
though frequently covered up with
a mass of hard and
almost impenetrable accretions,
is the spirit of Divine Love.*

– James Allen

Week #46

Love is the Truth of Your Being!

Love is the Truth of every human being, which belongs to the Supreme and which is real and immortal. While everything else changes and passes away, Love is permanent and imperishable.

Daily live in this Love and you will become fully conscious of its immortality here and now. Then you truly know your oneness with God for God is what Love is. You will know Love's divine and eternal nature. To know this is to know your own divine and eternal nature as a spiritual being.

This week's Love Positive Prayer: I am the Love that God is. Therefore I am divinely and eternally alive!

Declare the above prayer several times in the morning and at night. Centered in love, feel its joy and let it have free expression.

*Divine Love is the force
that dissolves all the opposers
of true thought and
thus smoothes out every obstacle
that presents itself.*

~ Charles Fillmore

Week #47

Divine Love Harmonizes Everything!

When Love rises up in your consciousness, it takes complete possession of your life and its rule is just and righteous. Even destructive faculties such as resistance, opposition, obstinacy, anger, and jealousy are harmonized through Love.

Perfect Love casts out all fear. When Love harmonizes your consciousness, you find that your outer affairs are put in order and where there seemed to be opposition and fear, cooperation and trust prevail.

This week's Love Positive Prayer: Centered in Divine Love, I am happy, healthy and free!

Declare the above prayer several times in the morning and at night. Consciously centered in Divine Love, feel its joy and experience its ecstasy!

*The moment we recognize
ourselves as one with
the Spirit of Infinite Love,
we become so filled with love
that we see only the good in all.*

– Ralph Waldo Trine

Week #48

We Are All One

When you realize that we are all one with Infinite Spirit, then you realize that in a real sense we are all one with each other. When you come into recognition of this fact, you can then do no harm to anyone or to anything. You realize that we are all members of one great body, that we are all connected with each other.

When you understand the reality of the oneness of all life that we are all dependent upon, the one Divine Source, then you let go of prejudice and all sense of separation. Love rules supreme and you and everyone lives together in harmony and peace.

This week's Love Positive Prayer: Through the Spirit of Infinite Love, I am unified and in harmony with all people.

Declare the above prayer several times in the morning and at night. Feel your complete oneness and harmony with everyone and everything.

You have all the love you need for healing, prosperity, and happy human relationships right within yourself.

– Catherine Ponder

Week #49

Divine Love is Your Success Power!

You needn't seek outside yourself for love. The good news is that you can begin releasing it from within yourself through your thoughts, words, actions and positive prayers*. As you do, you experience its great success power in its completeness as it works through people, situations, and conditions,

Realize now that Love is within you and consciously radiate it from you to everyone and everything. By so doing, you will become master of every condition and situation in your life. Everything and everybody will respond in a beautiful way and you will attract to you great success.

This week's Love Positive Prayer: Divine Love is my Success Power!

Declare the above prayer several times in the morning and at night. Feel your complete oneness and harmony with everyone and everything.

*Refer to the author's book, *Positive Prayer*.

131

Love yourself,
and you will grow in spirit.
To see, to hear, to know
and understand;
The message of the stars,
you shall hear it,
And all God's joys shall be
at your command.

-- Ella Wheeler Wilcox

Week #50

Love is Everything and Everybody!

Love your neighbor. Love yourself since you are the one closest to you. When you go to sleep at night and when you awaken each morning, send a thought of love into your whole being and out to the world. When you sincerely love everything and everybody, you will be amazed at the results because love is a magnet that attracts only the best to you.

Love and praise your body, think of it as a wonderful instrument of God and it will respond to your uplifted thought concerning it. Love and praise everyone and they will respond positively to you. Love and praise everything and your world will be magnificently alive with joy and happiness!

This week's Love Positive Prayer: I love myself and everyone and everything.

Declare the above prayer several times in the morning and at night. Feel your complete oneness and harmony with everyone and everything.

*Follow the path of love,
and all things are added,
for God is love,
and God is supply.*

– Florence Scovell Shinn

Week #51

Walk in Love

All disease and unhappiness come from failing to comply with the Law of Love. If you hate, resent, or criticize, it comes back to you laden with sickness and sorrow. When you love and praise, it comes back to you in good health, harmony and happiness.

A woman complained about her employer, who she said, was cold and critical toward her, and she knew she was not wanted in that position. She was told to behold the divinity in her employer and to send her love. When she did this, her employer became kind and supportive. Miracles happen, and keep on happening, when you walk in love!

This week's Love Positive Prayer: I walk in love and my life is happy and wonderful!

Declare the above prayer several times in the morning and at night. Feel your complete oneness and harmony with everyone and everything.

*If you would have
all the world love you,
you must first love
all the world.*

– Ralph Waldo Trine

Week #52

"Dear Everybody: I Love You!"

To the degree that you love, you will be loved. Thoughts are forces of creative energy. Each creates of its kind. Each one comes back energized with the effect that corresponds to itself and of which it is the cause. There is no better practice than to continually hold yourself in an attitude of mind that continuously sends out love.

It is a good practice to declare: "Dear Everybody: I Love You!" When you realize the fact that a thought invariably produces its effect before it returns, you can see how you are continually breathing out a blessing upon everybody, and the world. These same thoughts of love continually come back to you from everybody, and you are richly blessed.

This week's Love Positive Prayer: Dear Everybody: I Love You!

Declare the above prayer several times in the morning and at night. Feel your complete oneness and harmony with everyone and everything.

THE ONLY PLACE where Love can exist, as far as you are concerned, is in your own heart. Any love that is not in your heart does not exist for you.

The thing for you to do, then, is to fill your own heart with love by thinking it, feeling it, and expressing it; and when this sense of love is vivid enough it will heal you and solve your problems, and it will enable you to heal others, too.

This is the Law of Being and none of us can change it. – Emmet Fox

*   *   *

A special word of thanks. - I am grateful for the many friends whose love and tithes helped me establish Golden Key Ministry-Unity and who financially support our Prayer Ministry. Thank you for your past financial giving and for all that you continue to give. I am grateful for the readers of my books who write to me and who give special tithes in support of my ministry. Thank you! You are loved and appreciated! – *John Wolcott Adams*

Conclusion

Thank you for purchasing this book. I trust you use it as intended, as a daily, weekly focus on Divine Love to raise your consciousness and to live the Truth of your being. There is an old song that says, "What the world needs now is love, sweet love". But this is not wholly true. What the world needs now are more people like you who are growing in their awareness and acceptance of Divine Love as their reality, as well as knowing that this is the reality of everyone else.

The real way to create peace, individually and collectively, is through thinking on Love and dedicating ourselves to truly being the Love that we are.

I will be grateful to hear how this book has made a difference in your life. Kindly write to me. I love to hear good news!

John Wolcott Adams
Golden Key Ministry-Unity
P O Box 30989
Phoenix, AZ 85046 USA

RevJohn@GoldenKeyMinistry.com

Divine Love is simply love in its original purest form. Divine Love feels light and freeing. Divine Love encompasses you like a warm blanket giving you the feeling of protection and security. Divine Loves asks nothing of you but gives all. Divine Love feels complete; with Divine Love all yearning ceases and true happiness and contentment are realized.

- Rev. Doina Marie Barkhaus